discover countries

Discover
Iran

Rosie Wilson

PowerKiDS press.

New York

Published in 2012 by the Rosen Publishing Group, Inc.
29 East 21st Street, New York, NY 10010

First Edition

Concept Design: Jason Billin
Editors: Nicola Edwards and Kelly Davis
Designer: Amy Sparks
Picture Research: Amy Sparks
Consultant: Elaine Jackson

Photographs:
Cover (right) Dreamstime/Monica Boorboor; cover (left) Dreamstime/Massimiliano Lamagna; 1, Dreamstime/Stefan Baum; 3 (top), Dreamstime/Stefan Estvanik; 3 (bottom), Shutterstock/javarman; 4 (map), Stefan Chabluk; 5, Dreamstime/Stefan Baum; 6, Dreamstime/Delara; 7, Dreamstime/Valery Shanin; 8, Corbis/Ed Kashi; 9, Dreamstime/Sthlmfist; 10, Photolibrary/Paul Nevin; 11, Dreamstime/Valery Shanin; 12, Photolibrary/Kamran Jebreili; 13, Corbis/Christophe Boisvieux; 14, Corbis/Bruno Morandi/Hemis; 15, Shutterstock/javarman; 16, Art Directors; 17, Dreamstime/Monica Boorboor; 18, Corbis/Ahmed Jadallah/Reuters; 19, Photolibrary/Tony Waltham; 20, Dreamstime/Alexei Averianov; 21, Dreamstime/Steve Estvanik; 22 Photolibrary/Paul Nevin; 23, Shutterstock/Anna Rogal; 24, Alamy/David Young-Wolff; 25, Dreamstime/Artography; 26, Dreamstime/Orionna; 27, Alamy/Roger Parkes; 28, Corbis/Abedin Taherkenareh/epa/; 29, Dreamstime/Smellme.

Library of Congress Cataloging-in-Publication Data

Wilson, Rosie.
 Discover Iran / by Rosie Wilson. — 1st ed.
    p. cm. — (Discover countries)
 Includes index.
 ISBN 978-1-4488-6624-3 (library binding) — ISBN 978-1-4488-7050-9 (pbk.) —
 ISBN 978-1-4488-7316-6 (6-pack)
 1. Iran—Juvenile literature. I. Title.
 DS254.75.W55 2012
 955—dc23
                        2011028894

Manufactured in Malaysia

CPSIA Compliance Information: Batch #WW2102PK: For Further Information contact Rosen Publishing, New York, New York at 1-800-237-9932

Contents

Landscape and Climate

Iran mainly consists of a high desert plateau, surrounded by mountains. The Caspian Sea and the Persian Gulf border Iran to the north and south. Iran controls several islands in the Persian Gulf.

A Changeable Climate

The weather varies throughout Iran. In the capital, Tehran, it tends to be mild in all four seasons. The surrounding northern and western regions have clear seasons with extreme hot and cold temperatures and snow-covered mountains. The central desert region and the south are mainly mild in winter but hot and humid in summer, with high temperatures of 113 °F (45 °C) in the southern city of Abadan.

DID YOU KNOW?
The highest mountain in Iran, Mount Damavand, standing 18,606 feet (5,671 m) tall, is also a volcano. It is said in one story to be the final resting place of Noah's Ark.

▼ The Elburz Mountains sit along the north of the Iranian plateau. They are made up of many, mostly inactive, volcanic peaks.

High Land

Iran's high plateau of salt deserts and marshes is around 5,000 feet (1,500 m) above sea level. Two mountain ranges run along the north and south of Iran. Mount Taftan, in the southern Zagros mountains, still emits gas and mud from its volcanic cone. Iran also experiences dangerous earthquakes. In 2003, the city of Bam in the east was struck by an earthquake which resulted in more than 25,000 deaths.

Water Sources

One-third of Iran's boundary is seacoast, but there is little surface water inland. There are some fertile valleys in Iran, but much of the land is dry wasteland. Irrigation from underground water is essential for farming. There is little rainfall, but snowfalls in mountainous areas feed the rivers every spring. The main rivers, including the longest river, the Sefid, run from the two main mountain ranges to the seas. Lake Urmia, the largest lake, covers 2,000 sq. miles (5,180 sq. km).

▶ There are many small, seasonal streams in Iran. Villagers also use underground water from springs and wells.

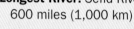

Facts at a Glance

Land Area: 591,352 sq. miles (1,531,595 sq. km)

Water Area: 45,020 sq. miles (116,600 sq. km)

Longest River: Sefid River 600 miles (1,000 km)

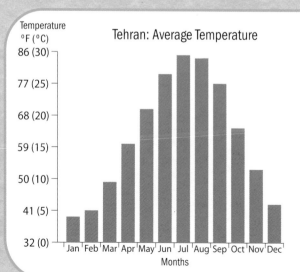

Temperature °F (°C)

Tehran: Average Temperature

86 (30)
77 (25)
68 (20)
59 (15)
50 (10)
41 (5)
32 (0)

Jan Feb Mar Apr May Jun Jul Aug Sep Oct Nov Dec

Months

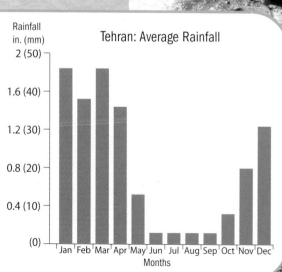

Rainfall in. (mm)

Tehran: Average Rainfall

2 (50)
1.6 (40)
1.2 (30)
0.8 (20)
0.4 (10)
(0)

Jan Feb Mar Apr May Jun Jul Aug Sep Oct Nov Dec

Months

Population and Health

In 2009, Iran had a population of around 74 million. This was more than triple what it had been 50 years earlier. Iran's population is growing more slowly now, but still increasing by nearly a million every year.

A Mixed Country

Different groups of people have been arriving and settling in the country since ancient times. Although the main ethnic group is mostly thought of as "the Persian people," Persian speakers actually include other groups, such as Turks, Arabs, Kurds, Armenians, and Jews.

Changing Population

In the last 30 years, refugees and asylum seekers have arrived in Iran from war-torn countries nearby, including Afghanistan and Iraq. There are now nearly 1 million Afghan refugees in Iran. The government recently tightened its controls on incoming refugees. There have been reports of people being deported, forced to relocate, or held in camps, sometimes against international laws.

Facts at a Glance

Total Population: 74.2 million

Life Expectancy at Birth: 71 years

Children Dying Before the Age of Five: 0.32%

Ethnic Composition: Persian 51%, Azeri 24%, Gilaki and Mazandarani 8%, Kurd 7%, Arab 3%, Lur 2%, Baloch 2%, Turkic 2%, other 1%

▼ This refugee camp near Khoy holds over 50,000 Kurdish refugees from Iraq. The camp has been here since the 1970s, as new Kurdish refugees continue to arrive in Iran.

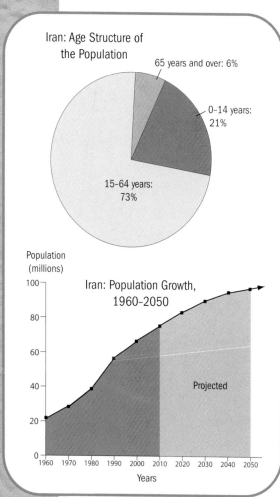

DID YOU KNOW?
On average, women live four years longer than men in Iran. A girl born in 2010 is expected to live 73 years, and a boy only 69 years.

◀ People protest in Sweden about an Iranian government election in 2009 that was declared unfair by international monitors. Some people choose to leave Iran to live in places where they feel they have more freedom.

Health and Life Expectancy

The main causes of death in Iran are diseases and accidents. Healthcare in Iran is good. Water quality is better than in the rest of the region. Today, Iran has a young population. The average age in the country is around 27. As good healthcare allows this population to grow old, there will be more elderly people overall.

Coping with More People

By 2050, the population in Iran is expected to reach nearly 100 million. This will mean larger, more heavily populated cities. There will also be more people who need education, healthcare, and employment. However, Iran has already coped with a rapidly increasing population, following the Revolution in 1979.

Iran: Age Structure of the Population

65 years and over: 6%

0–14 years: 21%

15–64 years: 73%

Population (millions)

Iran: Population Growth, 1960–2050

Projected

Years

Settlements and Living

Iran is increasingly an urban country. By 2009, more than 70 percent of the population lived in cities. Most major cities are located in the low regions near the borders of Iran, where the climate and soil are better. It is usually only nomadic people who live in the harshest areas, moving around to find milder conditions.

Cities

Around 7.9 million people live in Tehran, Iran's largest city and capital. Mashhad, the country's second-largest city, is also a major urban center. It is slightly larger than Chicago. Cities in Iran are divided into different sections. They have both modern skyscrapers and traditional central market areas, called bazaars, where people work and trade. Houses in urban areas often have a courtyard surrounded by a building, which stays cool on hot days. As the cities grew in the 1990s, housing for people with lower incomes was of a poorer quality. Since then, projects have been launched to improve the quality of houses for everyone in cities.

Facts at a Glance

Urban Population: 70% (52 million)

Rural Population: 30% (22.1 million)

Population of Largest City: 7.9 million (Tehran)

▼ Urban life in Iran is very similar to that in other parts of the world. People enjoy going to coffee and tea shops, shopping, and using cell phones and MP3 players.

Traditional Housing

Many people in Iran still live in rural areas. The mosque often marks the center of a village. People go there to study as well as to worship. A typical village on the plains forms a rectangular pattern, with the mosque in the middle. In contrast, nomadic peoples such as the Turkmen and Baloch have more temporary housing, such as huts or tents, called yurts. In the mountains, simple mud-brick dwellings protect people from the weather. In the milder and more fertile area near Caspian Sea, two-story houses are common, built with wood from the nearby forests.

◆ Village houses are built using both traditional and modern techniques and materials, depending on the materials available and the local environment.

DID YOU KNOW?

Iran's cities are growing at a rate of nearly 3,000 people every day. By 2050, 86 percent of Iranians will live in a city.

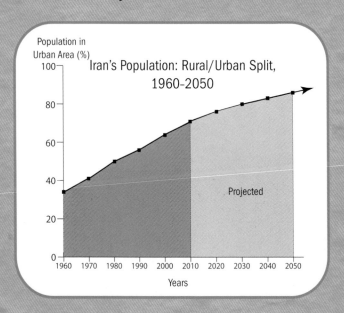

Population in
Urban Area (%)

Iran's Population: Rural/Urban Split, 1960–2050

100

80

60

40

Projected

20

0

1960 1970 1980 1990 2000 2010 2020 2030 2040 2050

Years

Family Life

The traditional family is still at the center of life in Iran, but this is beginning to change. Although the government prefers families to be headed by a man, often with several wives and children, young men and women in Iran today are campaigning for a more modern lifestyle.

The Role of the Family

After a population surge caused problems with housing and healthcare in the 1980s, the Ayatollah Khomeini, who led the Islamic Revolution in 1979, encouraged people to plan smaller families. Now, the average number of children per family is 1.7, instead of 6 or 7, as it had been 30 years ago.

Facts at a Glance

Average Children per Childbearing Woman:
1.7 children

Average Household Size:
4.1 people

Many Iranian weddings follow the tradition shown here of a meal eaten outdoors.

Families in Iran have been encouraged to leave time in between each child's birth and to have a maximum of three children to help control the population.

Children's Lives

Most children in Iran go to school, but they also help with cooking, cleaning, and other household chores. Rural children may help with farming work before and after school. Some, especially those in their teens, do not attend school at all. Some children in the cities earn money by shining shoes, cleaning windshields, or selling snacks.

Women in Iran

The Iranian government controls news in Iran, so it is sometimes difficult to find out about life there. Both positive and negative stories have emerged about Iranian women's lives, though. Unlike in most other countries, it is against the law for a woman to have a relationship with a man unless she is married to him. Women have been whipped or sentenced to death by stoning for having a relationship with a man, especially if they are already married to someone else. Women are legally obliged to cover their hair and dress modestly. They can also be punished for disobeying this law.

DID YOU KNOW?
Most Iranian girls used to get married at about 14. Since 1980, the average age has risen to around 21, but more and more women are choosing not to marry at all.

Religion and Beliefs

Religion is central to everyday life in Iran. A total of 89 percent of Iranians are Shia Muslims, but globally the Shia branch is a minority in Islam. Shia and Sunni Muslims separated in the seventh and eighth centuries because of many disagreements about who should become caliph, or religious leader, after the death of the Prophet Muhammad in 632 CE.

Theocratic Republic

Iran was declared an Islamic Republic during the Revolution in 1979. Strict laws were passed immediately, banning alcohol and Western music and controlling women's dress and behavior.

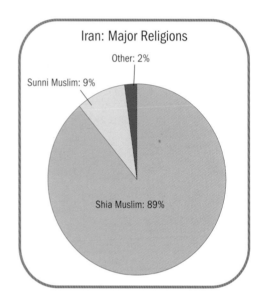

Iran: Major Religions

Other: 2%

Sunni Muslim: 9%

Shia Muslim: 89%

Male and female followers of Islam worship separately, in different areas of mosques.

The Islamic Republic of Iran is still governed by a Supreme Leader and a group of clerics, or scholars, who have studied Shi'ism. A man can be given the title of cleric if the rest of the clergy believe he understands the religion well enough to lead. Iran is the only Islamic state in the world with this type of government. The ruling clerics in the Assembly of Experts in Iran decide laws, justice, and the sentences for crimes, all based on traditional Sharia law, which is said to follow the will of Allah (God).

These buildings in the ancient city of Yazd, with their domes, arches, and towers, are beautiful examples of Islamic architecture.

Other Beliefs in Iran

Although Islam is the main faith, there are also Christians, Jews, and Zoroastrians living in Iran. Zoroastrianism is an Iranian religion from the time of the ancient Greeks. It combines belief in one God with magic and astrology. There are also followers of the Baha'i faith, a religion that started in Iran in 1844. Baha'is believe in combining all world religions and that every religious leader in the world has been God in human form. Three places in government, out of 290, are reserved for leaders of religious minorities.

DID YOU KNOW?
The Battle of Karbala, in which Shias were killed in their fight to decide the caliph, is commemorated every year. Iranians show respect by fasting and men beat themselves in the streets.

Education and Learning

Most children in Iran go to school, where boys and girls are taught separately. People in Iran are generally more educated than people in the neighboring countries of Pakistan and Afghanistan. Some students complete their studies at universities and colleges. Others learn trades, such as business or agriculture. Learning about Islam is a large part of education.

Mosque School

Most children attend primary school. Over 30 percent go to secondary school. At mosque schools, called madrassas, children learn about the five pillars of Islam. These are declaring your belief, praying, fasting during Ramadan, paying a religious tax, and completing a pilgrimage, or hajj, to Mecca during your lifetime.

Learning in the Army

All young men in Iran must do 18 months of military service. Most do this at the age of 19, although boys can join some forces when they are 15. Strict education continues for these soldiers. The military aims to make sure that Iran stays an Islamic Republic. It trains soldiers to help the Iranian people follow its laws.

⬥ This boy is completing his homework outside his father's shop in Esfahan.

Facts at a Glance

Children in Primary School:
Male 91%, Female 100%
Children in Secondary School:
Male 45%, Female 32%
Literacy Rate (Over 15 Years):
77%

Universities

After the revolution, many university professors had to leave their jobs in Iran because they did not support the government. Because of this, there are not enough university teachers. Iranians often attend universities overseas.

Some Iranians choose to stay in countries with less strict laws. Educated people have had problems in Iran since before the revolution, because they have often wanted the country to modernize its laws and their views are against those of the government. University education in Iran is improving. There are many courses available. Most graduates study the humanities or engineering.

▼ In one project in Iran, according to UNICEF, some schools are running weekly after-school classes with the schoolgirls themselves supervising the activities.

Employment and Economy

Iran holds about 10 percent of the world's oil reserves, or oil lying underground. In the last 30 years, its economy has grown and shrunk along with the global price of oil. The oil industry has brought wealth and jobs to Iran, but not everyone shares these benefits.

Money and Independence

When the revolutionary government came to power in 1979, it was unhappy with Iran's close links with the USA and it set about making Iran economically independent. This led to more employment opportunities and many people left rural farming areas to seek jobs in cities.

Facts at a Glance

Contributions to GDP:
Agriculture: 11%
Industry: 45%
Services: 44%
Labor Force:
Agriculture: 25%
Industry: 31%
Services: 44%
Female Labor Force:
30% of total
Unemployment Rate: 12%

▼ Small-scale farmers sell their produce at a local market in southern Iran.

Jobs and Services

Today only a quarter of working Iranians farm (compared to about 40 percent in 1979), and about a third do industrial work in factories, oil production, or mining. The service sector provides the most jobs, including those in schools, hospitals, and stores. The government is a large employer, as it owns the banks, insurance companies, and energy and water companies, as well as the telephone and television companies.

About a third of women (more than in many other Middle Eastern nations) are employed and this proportion is increasing. However, women still suffer many inequalities, including lower pay, fewer workers' rights, and some harassment.

Unemployment

Iran's unemployment rate is 12 percent. This is higher than in the USA, India, and the UK. Some Iranians are very poorly paid. Between 1990 and 2005, 7 percent of the population was living on less than $2 a day. The Ministry of Welfare is in charge of reducing poverty. Recent reforms have introduced new cash payments for the poorer members of Iran's population, but some welfare experts in Iran say that the government should do more. Many educated Iranians leave Iran to work in other countries, in search of a better quality of life.

○ These women work in the Iranian interior ministry in Tehran.

DID YOU KNOW?

Unlike banks in Western countries, banks in Iran are banned from charging fees on money borrowed from them, because it is against the religion of Islam.

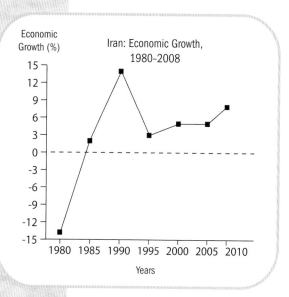

Economic Growth (%)

Iran: Economic Growth, 1980–2008

Years

Industry and Trade

Iran has avoided trading with wealthy Western countries, such as the USA, since the Islamic Revolution. It only trades with certain countries in the nearby region, such as the United Arab Emirates (UAE), or other world powers that also stand independent of the USA.

The Energy Industry

Iran is the world's second-largest producer of oil and natural gas. The country also produces more electricity than it needs. The government-controlled National Iranian Oil Company supervises most petroleum extraction and many oil refineries near major cities in Iran.

This Iranian oil storage facility is overshadowed by vast mountains. Iran also stores its crude oil in a fleet of supertankers in the Persian Gulf.

This woman is weaving a Persian carpet, which is an important Iranian export that is still popular throughout the world as a symbol of Persian history. There are an estimated 1.2 million carpet weavers in Iran.

Local Industry

Manufacturing in Iran has grown in the last 50 years. The country now produces a wide range of items, including cars, electrical appliances, phones, machinery, paper, rubber products, steel, food products, wood and leather goods, textiles, and pharmaceuticals. Most of these goods are sold in Iran's major cities.

Trading

Iran has become more independent from Western countries in the last 30 years, but Iranians still need to import many items. These vary from food products to manufactured goods, although some cultural items, such as Western music and movies, are banned. Along with oil, Iran also exports fruit, nuts, and crafts.

International Problems

There has been a major disagreement between the Iranian government and other nations about Iran's nuclear capability. The government of Iran says it is developing nuclear technology for use in generating energy for the Iranian people. However, some countries, such as the USA, fear that Iran is developing nuclear weapons.

Iran has also been accused of supporting Hezbollah and the Taliban, two terrorist groups that have been responsible for the deaths of many civilians in countries across the world. This possible link with international terrorism has led Western nations to enforce more sanctions against Iran, making trade very difficult.

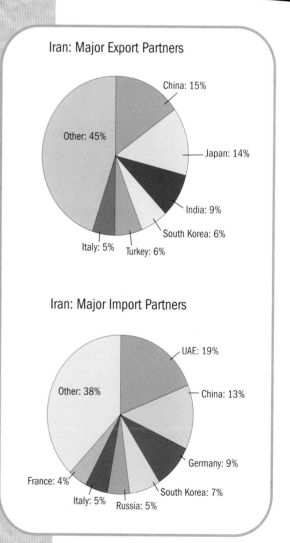

Iran: Major Export Partners

China: 15%
Japan: 14%
India: 9%
South Korea: 6%
Turkey: 6%
Italy: 5%
Other: 45%

Iran: Major Import Partners

UAE: 19%
China: 13%
Germany: 9%
South Korea: 7%
Russia: 5%
Italy: 5%
France: 4%
Other: 38%

Farming and Food

Farming in Iran now produces 11 percent of the country's national income. Although far fewer people farm now than they did 30 years ago, Iran still relies on locally produced food. Some luxury crops are important national exports, too.

Rural Decline

Much of Iran's soil is poor, making large-scale farming difficult. In addition, farms are often small, family-run, and not very profitable. These are some of the reasons why many people have left farms to find work in urban areas.

Facts at a Glance

Farmland:
30% of total land area

Main Agricultural Exports:
Pistachios, raisins, dates, wheat

Main Agricultural Imports:
Corn, soy bean oil, palm oil, rice, sugar

Average Daily Calorie Intake: 3,040

▼ Farm workers near Astara, on the coast of the Caspian Sea, harvest rice using traditional tools.

Fishing

Fishing is popular on both coastlines. Sturgeon are caught in Caspian Sea because their eggs, known as caviar, are a highly prized luxury food. The sturgeon are traditionally wild, although they are now sometimes farmed. After their eggs are extracted, the fish are often released to produce more roe, or eggs. Caviar is a key export for Iran.

Many Crops

Most of the food produced in Iran is sold within the country. Very little food is exported and only a small amount is imported. The main crops include vegetables and cereals, such as wheat, barley, rice, and corn. Fruits, such as dates, figs, pomegranates, melons, and grapes, are important crops, too. Cotton is also grown, as well as sugar beets and sugarcane, nuts, olives, spices, tea, tobacco, and medicinal herbs.

Iranian Food

Herding is also an important part of Iranian life and dairy products (mostly made from the milk of sheep and goats) are central to the Iranian diet. Food varies in the different regions, but rice and flatbreads are eaten everywhere. Meat, mostly lamb, is common. It is often eaten in a stew flavored with herbs, such as mint, and spices, such as saffron and turmeric. Alcohol is forbidden in Iran, but tea served black in glasses is popular.

▼ Tea is traditionaly served with a dish of pastries in a glass called an *ormud*. It is presented on a small patterned cloth called a *qalamkar*.

Transportation and Communications

Transportation and communications in Iran have been modernized over the last 20 years. Air travel has become common. As in other countries, people use cell phones and social networking, but these are all largely controlled by the Iranian government. Iranians have limited freedom to communicate.

Facts at a Glance

Total Roads: 107,452 miles (172,927 km)

Paved Roads: 78,236 miles (125,908 km)

Major Airports: 68

Major Ports: 3

Communication and Censorship

Cell phone ownership in Iran grew quickly in the 2000s. The use of the Internet also grew. These developments have eased the flow of information between Iran and the rest of the world. However, the Iranian government believes that Western ideas are damaging to Iranians. It therefore censors Internet communication and stops some cell phone videos from being sent.

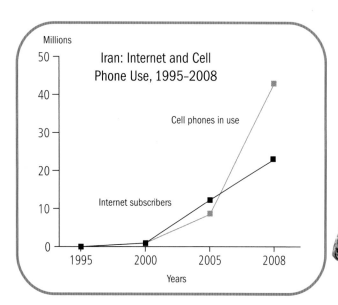

Iran: Internet and Cell Phone Use, 1995–2008

Millions

Cell phones in use

Internet subscribers

Years

▶ More than one in four people in Iran now owns a cell phone.

This is quite easy for the government, as it owns or controls most newspapers, TV news channels, and the national e-mail service. Sometimes the Iranian government stops people such as journalists and human rights workers from travelling to, or within, Iran.

Transportation in Iran

Iran's mountainous and desert areas make travelling difficult. Buses and trucks carry people and cargo between the main cities. Boats are used on the large Karun River. Iran Air provides flights between cities, as well as to many international destinations. Railroads also link the major cities and are used by some to travel through the country from Middle Eastern states to Central Asia.

Urban Transportation

The main cities have their own bus networks. Tehran has a subway system with several lines. As Tehran has grown, the number of cars has increased rapidly, causing traffic problems. In 2010, the Iranian government started trying to reduce traffic and air pollution by giving people incentives to move to other cities.

DID YOU KNOW?
In 2010, the Iranian government announced that it would ban the Internet search engine Google. It would instead introduce a national e-mail service, to control the information flow between Iran and the rest of the world.

▶ Traffic is becoming a problem in Tehran, shown here in the distance. Overall, car ownership is still quite low in Iran compared to the USA or China, though.

Leisure and Tourism

As Iranians in the cities become wealthier, they have more money to spend on leisure activities, such as going to the movies and playing sports. International tourists also come to Iran. In 2008, about two million foreigners visited Iran's tourist attractions.

Persian History

Iran is famous for its Persian Empire, which ended when the Persians were conquered by Alexander the Great in the fourth century BCE. There are now 12 World Heritage sites in Iran, including the two capitals of the former empire, Persepolis and Pasargadae. They contain ruins of grand buildings and homes from the sixth and seventh centuries BCE.

⬇ Many tourists go to Iran each year to visit ruins from the Persian Empire, such as these columns in the ancient city of Persepolis.

Facts at a Glance

Tourist Arrivals (Millions)	
1995	0.5
2000	1.3
2005	1.9
2008	2.0

Some sites are even older, dating back to other ancient civilizations partly located in Iran, such as the Mesopotamian Empire and the Kingdom of Elam. Tourists visit both these historic sites and Iran's beaches, ski resorts, and beautiful mosques.

Celebration

Iran's main day of celebration is Nowruz. This is the New Year holiday and the birthday of the twelfth Imam. Nowruz is celebrated for a whole week, ending with a picnic. On the night before the last Wednesday of the old year, called Red Wednesday, people leap over bonfires to cast out the ill omens of the old year.

People enjoy boating on the Zayandeh River in Esfahan during the national holiday of Nowruz.

Culture

Iranian-made films have been praised by critics around the world. The government has not been able to control the film industry, but it does try to limit the films that are produced. The government is in favor of films that celebrate Iranian life. Films that seem too close to Western life or too critical of Iranian life are not officially screened in the country.

Sports, both traditional and modern, are also popular with Iranians. Many cheered on the Iranian soccer team in the 2010 World Cup, and soccer is widely played and watched. Traditional sports include wrestling and horse racing.

DID YOU KNOW?
TV is popular in Iran, but watching non-government TV is difficult, as international channels are often jammed or blocked to stop Iranians from watching them.

Environment and Wildlife

As Iran has developed, people's behavior has begun to have a negative impact on wildlife and the environment. The government is taking some steps to prevent this, but international experts think that countries with developing economies, such as Iran, need to invest in more renewable energy to avoid contributing to global CO_2 emissions.

Facts at a Glance

Proportion of Area Protected: 6.5%

Biodiversity (Known Species): 8,787

Threatened Species: 53

Environmental Damage

Since Iran has so much oil, it can make gasoline easily and cheaply. Therefore, the people of Iran have little motivation to reduce their car usage. Electricity use has also more than doubled in the last 15 years. Most of this comes from oil-burning power plants, which release more CO_2 and pollution into the atmosphere.

Air pollution in Tehran sometimes rises to dangerous levels, causing offices and schools to close.

Wildlife

A huge variety of plants and animals exist in Iran. Different species live in each region. In desert areas, there are shrubs and bushes. There are also oases where date palms and acacia trees grow. Desert animals include rabbits, deer, onagers, rodents, and birds of prey, such as buzzards. In the mountains and forests, there are leopards, hyenas, bears, wild boars, and gazelles. Seabirds live in the coastal areas and over 200 varieties of fish and some shellfish live in the Persian Gulf.

Protection

The government has established national parks and protected areas to protect the wildlife of Iran. Endangered species include the Kaiser's spotted newt and, in the Caspian region, the rare Asian cheetah. The government has also banned the hunting of some species of swans, deer, and pheasants. There were once tigers in Iran, but they are now thought to be extinct.

⬯ The onager is still found in Iran's deserts but is now critically endangered.

DID YOU KNOW?

It is thought that there are only 100 Asian cheetahs left in the wild in Iran. In ancient times, cheetahs were trained by kings to hunt gazelles.

Glossary

astrology (uh-STRAH-luh-jee) The belief that the stars and the planets affect life on Earth.

ayatollah (eye-uh-TOH-luh) Important religious leader for Shia Muslims.

campaigning (kam-PAY-ning) Working for a certain result, such as winning an election.

censor (SEN-ser) To take out parts of something to keep others for seeing them.

cleric (KLER-ik) A religious leader who has had official religious training.

commemorate (kuh-MEH-muh-rayt) To remember officially.

deport (dih-PORT) To send out of a country.

emit (ee-MIT) To put a gas or other substance into the air.

fertile (FER-tul) Good for making and growing things.

herding (HURD-ing) Gathering animals and making them move.

incentive (in-SEN-tiv) A reason or reward for doing something.

irrigation (ih-rih-GAY-shun) The carrying of water to land through ditches or pipes.

manufacturing (man-yuh-FAK-cher-ing) Making something by hand or with a machine.

military (MIH-luh-ter-ee) The armed forces of a country.

minorities (my-NOR-ih-tees) Groups of people that are in some way different from the larger part of a population.

mosque (MOSK) A place of worship and prayer for Muslims.

nomadic (noh-MA-dik) Roaming about from place to place.

nuclear technology (NOO-klee-ur tek-NAH-luh-jee) The knowledge and things needed to make energy or weapons by splitting tiny bits of matter called atoms.

peninsula (peh-NIN-suh-luh) An area of land surrounded by water on three sides.

petroleum extraction (peh-TROH-lee-um ek-STRAK-shun) Taking an oily liquid that can be used to make gasoline and other products out of the ground.

pilgrimage (PIL-gruh-mij) A journey to a sacred or godly place.

plateau (pla-TOH) A broad, flat, high piece of land.

procession (pruh-SEH-shun) A group of people moving along in an orderly way for a special purpose or occasion.

Ramadan (RAH-meh-don) The ninth month of the Muslim calendar, observed by daily fasting from sunrise to sunset.

refugees (reh-fyoo-JEEZ) People who leave their own countries to find safety.

republic (rih-PUH-blik) A form of government in which the authority belongs to the people.

revolution (reh-vuh-LOO-shun) A complete change in government.

sanctions (SANK-shuns) Measures taken by one country to try to make another country follow international rules or agreements. Sanctions are often limits on trading.

theocratic (thee-uh-KRA-tik) Having to do with a state which is led by religious leaders.

uranium (yoo-RAY-nee-um) A heavy metallic element that gives off rays of energy.

Topic Web

Use this topic web to explore Iranian themes
in different areas of your study.

Internet Technology
The American government does not encourage Americans to visit Iran. Use the Internet to find out why this is.

Citizenship
Do you think that people in Iran have the same rights as people in the USA? What are the main differences? Can you think of anything that people in Iran are not allowed to do that people in the USA are free to do?

History
Find out about how people lived in one of the ancient empires that Iran is famous for. You could choose Persia, Mesopotamia, or the Kingdom of Elam.

Design and Technology
Use the information on housing in villages in Iran to make some models of the different types of village houses.

Iran

Math
Iran's currency is the rial. Find out how many rials there are in $1, $5, and $10.

Science
Extracting and refining oil is Iran's main industry. Find out what solids, liquids, and gases are involved in the oil extraction and refining processes.

English
Using pages 28–9, design and write an information factsheet describing the main animals and birds in Iran. Use the Internet to find more facts to include.

Geography
Iran shares borders with many other countries. Find out which region each of Iran's neighbors is considered to be a part of.

Further Reading, Web Sites, and Index

Further Reading

Iran by Walter Simmons (Bellwether Media, 2011)

Iran: A Primary Source Cultural Guide by Lauren Spencer (Rosen Publishing, 2004)

Iran: The People by April Fast (Crabtree Publishing Company, 2010)

Web Sites

Due to the changing nature of Internet links, PowerKids Press has developed an online list of Web sites related to the subject of this book. This site is updated regularly. Please use this link to access the list: www.powerkidslinks.com/discovc/iran/

Index